VIOLIN

101 JAZZ SONGS

Available for
FLUTE, CLARINET, ALTO SAX, TENOR SAX, TRUMPET,
HORN, TROMBONE, VIOLIN, VIOLA, CELLO

ISBN 978-1-4950-2344-6

HAL•LEONARD®
CORPORATION

7777 W. BLUEMOUND RD. P.O. BOX 13819 MILWAUKEE, WI 53213

Visit Hal Leonard Online at
www.halleonard.com

CONTENTS

ALL OF ME

VIOLIN

Words and Music by SEYMOUR SIMONS
and GERALD MARKS

ALL THE THINGS YOU ARE

VIOLIN

Lyrics by OSCAR HAMMERSTEIN II
Music by JEROME KERN

APRIL IN PARIS

VIOLIN

Words by E.Y. "YIP" HARBURG
Music by VERNON DUKE

AUTUMN IN NEW YORK

VIOLIN

Words and Music by
VERNON DUKE

AUTUMN LEAVES

VIOLIN

English Lyric by JOHNNY MERCER
French Lyric by JACQUES PREVERT
Music by JOSEPH KOSMA

BEWITCHED

Violin

Words by LORENZ HART
Music by RICHARD RODGERS

BEYOND THE SEA

Lyrics by JACK LAWRENCE
Music by CHARLES TRENET and ALBERT LASRY
Original French Lyric to "La Mer" by CHARLES TRENET

VIOLIN

THE BLUE ROOM

Violin

Words by LORENZ HART
Music by RICHARD RODGERS

BLUE SKIES

VIOLIN

Words and Music by
IRVING BERLIN

BLUESETTE

VIOLIN

Words by NORMAN GIMBEL
Music by JEAN THIELEMANS

Medium Jazz Waltz

BODY AND SOUL

VIOLIN

Words by EDWARD HEYMAN,
ROBERT SOUR and FRANK EYTON
Music by JOHN GREEN

BUT BEAUTIFUL

Violin

Words by JOHNNY BURKE
Music by JIMMY VAN HEUSEN

CAN'T HELP LOVIN' DAT MAN

VIOLIN

Lyrics by OSCAR HAMMERSTEIN II
Music by JEROME KERN

Moderately and rather freely, with a lilt

CARAVAN

VIOLIN

Words and Music by DUKE ELLINGTON,
IRVING MILLS and JUAN TIZOL

CHARADE

VIOLIN

By HENRY MANCINI

CHEEK TO CHEEK

VIOLIN

Words and Music by
IRVING BERLIN

COME RAIN OR COME SHINE

VIOLIN

Words by JOHNNY MERCER
Music by HAROLD ARLEN

DANCING ON THE CEILING

VIOLIN

Words by LORENZ HART
Music by RICHARD RODGERS

DEARLY BELOVED

VIOLIN

Music by JEROME KERN
Words by JOHNNY MERCER

DO NOTHIN' TILL YOU HEAR FROM ME

Violin

Words and Music by DUKE ELLINGTON
and BOB RUSSELL

DON'T GET AROUND MUCH ANYMORE

VIOLIN

Words and Music by DUKE ELLINGTON
and BOB RUSSELL

DREAMSVILLE

Violin

By HENRY MANCINI

FALLING IN LOVE WITH LOVE

Violin

Words by LORENZ HART
Music by RICHARD RODGERS

Moderate Waltz tempo

A FINE ROMANCE

Violin

Words by DOROTHY FIELDS
Music by JEROME KERN

FLY ME TO THE MOON
(In Other Words)

VIOLIN

Words and Music by
BART HOWARD

GEORGIA ON MY MIND

VIOLIN

Words by STUART GORRELL
Music by HOAGY CARMICHAEL

HERE'S THAT RAINY DAY

VIOLIN

Words by JOHNNY BURKE
Music by JIMMY VAN HEUSEN

HERE'S TO LIFE

VIOLIN

Music by ARTIE BUTLER
Lyrics by PHYLLIS MOLINARY

HONEYSUCKLE ROSE

VIOLIN

Words by ANDY RAZAF
Music by THOMAS "FATS" WALLER

HOW DEEP IS THE OCEAN
(How High Is the Sky)

VIOLIN

Words and Music by
IRVING BERLIN

HOW INSENSITIVE
(Insensatez)

Music by ANTONIO CARLOS JOBIM
Original Words by VINICIUS DE MORAES
English Words by NORMAN GIMBEL

VIOLIN

Medium Bossa Nova

I CAN'T GET STARTED

VIOLIN

Words by IRA GERSHWIN
Music by VERNON DUKE

I COULD WRITE A BOOK

VIOLIN

Words by LORENZ HART
Music by RICHARD RODGERS

I GOT IT BAD AND THAT AIN'T GOOD

Violin

Words by PAUL FRANCIS WEBSTER
Music by DUKE ELLINGTON

I'LL REMEMBER APRIL

VIOLIN

Words and Music by PAT JOHNSTON,
DON RAYE AND GENE DE PAUL

I'M BEGINNING TO SEE THE LIGHT

Violin

Words and Music by DON GEORGE, JOHNNY HODGES, DUKE ELLINGTON and HARRY JAMES

Medium Bounce

I'VE GOT THE WORLD ON A STRING

VIOLIN

Words by TED KOEHLER
Music by HAROLD ARLEN

IF I WERE A BELL

VIOLIN

By FRANK LOESSER

IMAGINATION

VIOLIN

Words by JOHNNY BURKE
Music by JIMMY VAN HEUSEN

IN A SENTIMEMTAL MOOD

Violin

By DUKE ELLINGTON

IN THE WEE SMALL HOURS OF THE MORNING

VIOLIN

Words by BOB HILLIARD
Music by DAVID MANN

Slowly

INDIANA
(Back Home Again in Indiana)

VIOLIN

Words by BALLARD MacDONALD
Music by JAMES F. HANLEY

Moderately, with a lilt

ISN'T IT ROMANTIC?

VIOLIN

Words by LORENZ HART
Music by RICHARD RODGERS

IT COULD HAPPEN TO YOU

VIOLIN

Words by JOHNNY BURKE
Music by JAMES VAN HEUSEN

IT DON'T MEAN A THING

(If It Ain't Got That Swing)

Violin

Words and Music by DUKE ELLINGTON
and IRVING MILLS

IT MIGHT AS WELL BE SPRING

VIOLIN

Lyrics by OSCAR HAMMERSTEIN II
Music by RICHARD RODGERS

THE LADY IS A TRAMP

VIOLIN

Words by LORENZ HART
Music by RICHARD RODGERS

LAZY RIVER

VIOLIN

Words and Music by HOAGY CARMICHAEL
and SIDNEY ARODIN

Moderate Swing

LIKE SOMEONE IN LOVE

VIOLIN

Words by JOHNNY BURKE
Music by JIMMY VAN HEUSEN

LITTLE GIRL BLUE

VIOLIN

Words by LORENZ HART
Music by RICHARD RODGERS

LONG AGO (AND FAR AWAY)

Words by IRA GERSHWIN
Music by JEROME KERN

LOVER, COME BACK TO ME

VIOLIN

Lyrics by OSCAR HAMMERSTEIN II
Music by SIGMUND ROMBERG

LULLABY OF BIRDLAND

Violin

Words by GEORGE DAVID WEISS
Music by GEORGE SHEARING

LULLABY OF THE LEAVES

VIOLIN

Words by JOE YOUNG
Music by BERNICE PETKERE

MANHATTAN

VIOLIN

Words by LORENZ HART
Music by RICHARD RODGERS

MEDITATION
(Meditação)

VIOLIN

Music by ANTONIO CARLOS JOBIM
Original Words by NEWTON MENDONÇA
English Words by NORMAN GIMBEL

MIDNIGHT SUN

VIOLIN

Words and Music by LIONEL HAMPTON,
SONNY BURKE and JOHNNY MERCER

MISTY

VIOLIN

Music by ERROLL GARNER

Slowly, with a smooth Swing

MOOD INDIGO

Violin

Words and Music by DUKE ELLINGTON,
IRVING MILLS and ALBANY BIGARD

MOONLIGHT IN VERMONT

VIOLIN

Words by JOHN BLACKBURN
Music by KARL SUESSDORF

MORE THAN YOU KNOW

VIOLIN

Words by WILLIAM ROSE and EDWARD ELISCU
Music by VINCENT YOUMANS

Slowly, with expression

MY HEART STOOD STILL

VIOLIN

Words by LORENZ HART
Music by RICHARD RODGERS

MY OLD FLAME

VIOLIN

Words and Music by ARTHUR JOHNSTON
and SAM COSLOW

Moderate Swing

MY ONE AND ONLY LOVE

Violin

Words by ROBERT MELLIN
Music by GUY WOOD

MY ROMANCE

VIOLIN

Words by LORENZ HART
Music by RICHARD RODGERS

MY SHIP

VIOLIN

Words by IRA GERSHWIN
Music by KURT WEILL

THE NEARNESS OF YOU

VIOLIN

Words by NED WASHINGTON
Music by HOAGY CARMICHAEL

A NIGHT IN TUNISIA

VIOLIN

By JOHN "DIZZY" GILLESPIE
and FRANK PAPARELLI

ON GREEN DOLPHIN STREET

VIOLIN

Lyrics by NED WASHINGTON
Music by BRONISLAU KAPER

ONE NOTE SAMBA
(Samba de uma nota so)

VIOLIN

Original Lyrics by NEWTON MENDONÇA
English Lyrics by ANTONIO CARLOS JOBIM
Music by ANTONIO CARLOS JOBIM

Medium Bossa Nova

PICK YOURSELF UP

VIOLIN

Words by DOROTHY FIELDS
Music by JEROME KERN

POLKA DOTS AND MOONBEAMS

Violin

Words by JOHNNY BURKE
Music by JIMMY VAN HEUSEN

QUIET NIGHTS OF QUIET STARS
(Corcovado)

VIOLIN

English Words by GENE LEES
Original Words and Music by ANTONIO CARLOS JOBIM

Medium Bossa Nova

SATIN DOLL

VIOLIN

By DUKE ELLINGTON

SKYLARK

Violin

Words by JOHNNY MERCER
Music by HOAGY CARMICHAEL

SO NICE
(Summer Samba)

VIOLIN

Original Words and Music by MARCOS VALLE
and PAULO SERGIO VALLE
English Words by NORMAN GIMBEL

SOPHISTICATED LADY

Violin

Words and Music by DUKE ELLINGTON,
IRVING MILLS and MITCHELL PARISH

SPEAK LOW

VIOLIN

Words by OGDEN NASH
Music by KURT WEILL

Stella by Starlight

Violin

Words by NED WASHINGTON
Music by VICTOR YOUNG

STOMPIN' AT THE SAVOY

Violin

By BENNY GOODMAN,
EDGAR SAMPSON and CHICK WEBB

STORMY WEATHER
(Keeps Rainin' All the Time)

VIOLIN

Lyric by TED KOEHLER
Music by HAROLD ARLEN

A SUNDAY KIND OF LOVE

VIOLIN

Words and Music by LOUIS PRIMA, ANITA NYE LEONARD,
STANLEY RHODES and BARBARA BELLE

TANGERINE

Words by JOHNNY MERCER
Music by VICTOR SCHERTZINGER

VIOLIN

THERE'S A SMALL HOTEL

VIOLIN

Words by LORENZ HART
Music by RICHARD RODGERS

THESE FOOLISH THINGS (REMIND ME OF YOU)

VIOLIN

Words by HOLT MARVELL
Music by JACK STRACHEY

THE THINGS WE DID LAST SUMMER

VIOLIN

Words by SAMMY CAHN
Music by JULE STYNE

THIS CAN'T BE LOVE

Violin

Words by LORENZ HART
Music by RICHARD RODGERS

THOU SWELL

VIOLIN

Words by LORENZ HART
Music by RICHARD RODGERS

UNFORGETTABLE

VIOLIN

Words and Music by
IRVING GORDON

THE VERY THOUGHT OF YOU

VIOLIN

Words and Music by
RAY NOBLE

WATCH WHAT HAPPENS

VIOLIN

Music by MICHEL LEGRAND
Original French Text by JACQUES DEMY
English Lyrics by NORMAN GIMBEL

WAVE

VIOLIN

Words and Music by
ANTONIO CARLOS JOBIM

THE WAY YOU LOOK TONIGHT

Words by DOROTHY FIELDS
Music by JEROME KERN

Violin

WHAT'LL I DO

VIOLIN

Words and Music by
IRVING BERLIN

WILLOW WEEP FOR ME

VIOLIN

Words and Music by
ANN RONELL

WITCHCRAFT

Violin

Music by CY COLEMAN
Lyrics by CAROLYN LEIGH

YESTERDAYS

VIOLIN

Words by OTTO HARBACH
Music by JEROME KERN

YOU ARE TOO BEAUTIFUL

VIOLIN

Words by LORENZ HART
Music by RICHARD RODGERS

YOU BROUGHT A NEW KIND OF LOVE TO ME

VIOLIN

Words and Music by SAMMY FAIN,
IRVING KAHAL and PIERRE NORMAN

Medium Swing

YOU DON'T KNOW WHAT LOVE IS

VIOLIN

Words and Music by DON RAYE
and GENE DePAUL